Unlocked Diaries

For nothing is secret that shall not be made
manifest; neither anything hid, that shall not be
known and come abroad Luke 8:17

Copyright © 2021 Athena Goldsby

Published by

Living Water Book, Christian Division of Butterfly
Typeface Publishing House, Little Rock, Arkansas 72201

Livingwaterbooks.org

Print Book Edition 2022

ISBN 979-8-9868286-0-2

Graphics, Art, and Designs Living Water Books

John 7:38

He who believes in me, as the scripture has said,
Out of his heart will flow rivers of living water.

Poetry became healing for me.!!

ATHENA GOLDSBY

While reflecting on situations that have occurred in my life, I realized that life and love have taken me through many avenues. These various routes have inspired me to write this book to share with others. Now I am giving access to the world my well-kept innermost emotions, feelings, thoughts, and experiences. My hope is to share with others my writings with a goal to inspire, uplift, and encourage others all while edifying God.

I dedicate this book to God Almighty, the very being and source of my life, who has allowed the development and creation of this book.

Luke 8:16
"No one lights a lamp and hides it in a clay jar or puts it under a bed. Instead, they put it on a stand, so that those who come in can see the light."

Dedication

Acknowledgements

Steve & Darlene Goldsby,
my parents who nourished and loved me, taught me great morals in life
and kept me on the right path.

Nicole F. Morgan,
my cousin who has been there with me through nearly every moment of my
life; we have done so much together.
She would not let me give up on living life. I thank God for her.

Lucientus V. Goldsby (Katie),
my sister who loves me, and makes sure I am taken care of.
She is a tremendous giver. I love you!

Nastochia R. Dixon (NeNe),
my cousin who is like a sister to me. We have done so much together, and
over the years we (Nicole, Katie, and NeNe) have shared some intimate
things with each other. These are my girls.

Marcus Goldsby,
my brother who lives in California, and though we never see each other, he
makes sure to call; he encourages me never to give up because no matter my
physical disability, I can do anything. I love you, brother!

Jerome & Joy Goldsby,
my uncle and aunt who war in the spirit for myself and my family.
Thank you for pouring the word of God into my life.

Shannon Lewis, my cousin
always encourages me to let God be God in my life. He always encourages
me to go after my goals and dreams
and walk in my God-given talents.

≫Table of Contents

Dedication
Acknowledgements
Preface

09

Chapter One

- What is Young Love
- Sweet Peace
- I Love You

17

Chapter Two

- The Signs
- Choosy Love
- Love don't live here
- Anticipating
- Deception
- Despair
- You told me

34

Chapter Three

- Pray the storm away
- My Sister
- Reminiscing Jamal

Table of Contents

42

Chapter Four

- Experiencing Love
- Purposeful Love
- You Are
- To Love You
- Love Escapade
- Love

55

Chapter Five

- FindingPurpose
- Within
- Battle Within
- Suicide
- I am Somebody
- Dare to dream
- Anew
- Radiance
- God's Word
- Faith
- On The Wings of My Savior
- Everything
- When I found you

83

Conclusion

- Express Yourself Journal
- About The Author
- About The Publisher

Preface

This book contains poetry that has been written over the years of my life following a shooting incident that caused me to be confined to a wheelchair. I thought my life was, at that point, meaningless. I did not want to do anything in life; because I did not know what I could do. I felt confined in the body as well as in the mind because in neither was I being fruitful. I was lost and depressed at the age of fourteen. I received a birthday gift from a friend of mine and it was a journal. After writing my first poem, I felt joy, peace, and freedom.

My writings were flowing from a place within my heart. A place where I stored things that occurred in my life. The topics ranged from the shooting incident, dating, emotional stability, revelations from God, desiring to be loved, and spiritual growth. I pray you enjoy the gifts found within these pages. They truly are expressions of my soul.

Chapter One

Young Love

What is Young Love?

My first serious relationship began when I was in the 7th grade. We dated on and off until my freshman year in college. When I first showed interest in him, he blew me off because he was pursuing another girl, but I wanted to be his girl so bad. We eventually started dating.

When you're young, and experiencing this new kind of life... this thing called "love," you tend to be led by your feelings, instead of wisdom. "Young Love" is what it's called....young, and in love. I wonder if that is why it's called young love. So, the question is, "What is "young love?" Can Adults and those who have been married for years come back to this feeling, of young love?

Date _____

Journaling
Reflections

_____

_____

_____

_____

_____

_____

_____

_____

_____

I'm praying for ....

_____

Lord teach me to....

_____

Sweet Peace

The love you give is

S *entimental*

W *onderful*

E *rotic*

E *xotic*

T *ender*

What I see when I look into your eyes

P *assion*

E *ndearment*

A *ffection*

C *harm*

E *ndless Love*

Date _____

Journaling
Reflections

_____

_____

_____

_____

_____

_____

_____

_____

_____

_____

I'm praying for ....

_____

Lord teach me to....

_____

Many young couples who are in love have the mindset that they are going to be together forever. I'll never forget the conversation that me and my first love had one day on the topic of being together forever. I asked him would he still be with me if I was in a wheelchair. Lo and behold, this very situation occurred.

I just began my sophomore year of high school. It was an early morning in September, September 8, 1998 to be exact. I was asleep in bed with my mom and dad when about four young men entered our home. One of them opened fire, striking me and my mom. This incident resulted in me being paralyzed from the waist down. My first love and I continued to date for the next two to three years, on and off.

So the question is, "Is it silly when you are young and in love to think or even hope that you and your love will be together forever?"

ATHENA GOLDSBY

I Love You

If I had one wish, I would wish to be with you.

If I had one promise, I would promise to be true.

I cannot guarantee that we will be together forever,

because I know one day, we will have to part.

But no matter the situation, you will always be in my heart.

I feel for you something I've never felt.

It's like I'm the snow,

and you're the sun causing me to melt.

I hope you take me seriously because I'm honestly being true.

So, please believe every word I say when I say, "I love you."

Date _____

Journaling
Reflections

_____

_____

_____

_____

_____

_____

_____

_____

_____

I'm praying for ....

_____

Lord teach me to....

_____

Chapter Two

Toxic Relationships

The Signs

A toxic relationship makes you feel unsupported,
misunderstood, demeaned, and attacked.
The signs of a toxic relationship
are lack of support, toxic communication,
envy, jealousy, and controlling behaviors.
There's resentment, dishonesty, patterns of disrespect,
and negative financial behaviors.
Pay attention to the signs.

Date _____

Journaling
Reflections

_____

_____

_____

_____

_____

_____

_____

_____

_____

I'm praying for ....

_____

Lord teach me to....

_____

Choosy Lover

When all of your insides

are telling you that he isn't the one for you,

yet you ignore it, and ignore all the signs too.

My, my, my ...

You better choose wisely!

Date _____

Journaling
Reflections

_____

_____

_____

_____

_____

_____

_____

_____

_____

_____

I'm praying for ....

_____

Lord teach me to....

_____

Love don't Live here

He took my heart. Now he's gone.
He left me and did me wrong.

I was blind and could not see
that he was cheating on me.

While all this time I was fooling myself,
he was out with someone else.

I heard much talk from my friends,
but I didn't pay it no mind
because I was blind.

All the schemes, all the lies,
you couldn't look me in the eyes

You were my love, my #1 Boo,
but you misused me and abused the truth.

Now your love lives here no more.

Date _____

Journaling
Reflections

_____

_____

_____

_____

_____

_____

_____

_____

_____

_____

I'm praying for ....

_____

Lord teach me to....

_____

*So, now that happened, and he apologized.
For whatever reasons, I continued to be with him,
and for whatever reasons, he continues to cheat,
and this becomes a cycle. At some point, my first love
relationship became quite tumultuous. We would
physically fight.*

The question is, "Is this normal?"

Is this what love looks like or even feels like?

ATHENA GOLDSBY

Anticipating

Sitting up at night,

every second and every minute,

hoping you're about to walk through the door.

Still every second and every minute turns into hours.

The silence begins to overwhelm me becoming unbearable,

You become so distant...far away.

With every second and every minute

I realize I am alone.

In the darkness of my room

I see images all around me of what could be.

Date _____

Journaling
Reflections

_____

_____

_____

_____

_____

_____

_____

_____

_____

I'm praying for ....

_____

Lord teach me to....

_____

Deception

Clothed in the unseen,

living the unreal... Deception.

Lies that are so beautiful,

painting a faux picture... Deception.

Hidden from the visible eye.

Sweet lies told by the fireside.

Mysteries burned within, never to be revealed.

Hearts are broken, the truth is never spoken.

Identity lost, humanity was the cost.... Deception.

Strawman, Strawman, make the fire hotter!

Rise up fire, rise up fire.

Strawman, strawman,

feeding me fodder of lies... Deception.

Date _____

Journaling
Reflections

_____

_____

_____

_____

_____

_____

_____

_____

_____

I'm praying for ....

_____

Lord teach me to....

_____

How long must I experience heartache and pain?

I would say that it's just a reality...
Yes, every man cheats, and that's
the way it is. It seemed that the cheating
would never cease.

I thought my first love was unfaithful to me
because I was in a wheelchair. I began blaming
myself for his actions, which led to me becoming
depressed and hating that I was in a wheelchair.

ATHENA GOLDSBY

Despair

All of loves loss, All of loves hope,
People able to look on to another day
but the unfortunate ones, the hurt ones,
are grieving in despair,

Without the hope of finding another love,
find themselves in the gutter,
shut out in the cold.
No one knows my sorrow,
and no one knows my misfortune.

As I live each day without you in my life,
my heart decays.
Soon there will be no remains.
I see you; I smell you; I feel you; I live you.
Only I know the wonders of you.

Is it a sin to love you this much?

Date _____

Journaling
Reflections

_____

_____

_____

_____

_____

_____

_____

_____

_____

I'm praying for ....

_____

Lord teach me to....

_____

You Told Me

You told me that you love me,

but I don't quite understand.

You told me that you want to be with me,

to have this great romance.

You said that we will be together forever,

forever it's you and me,

but as time went by,

we became nothing more

than just a memory.

Date _____

Journaling
Reflections

_____

_____

_____

_____

_____

_____

_____

_____

_____

_____

I'm praying for ....

_____

Lord teach me to....

_____

Chapter Three

Encouragment
and Inspiration

Pray The Storm Away

It began with claps of thunder

ringing aloud in my ears, shaking my soul.

The stroke of lightning, I see in your eyes, blazing fiercely.

The winds begin to blow, hot and humid,

bringing showers of rain.

The water rises and the wind causes waves to form.

They begin to overtake me, tossing me to and fro.

I stretch my arms out to grasp you,

and my heart is pounding from the fear of losing you.

I don't want this storm to be the death of me.

I close my eyes and pray for God's unfailing hand

to reach in and pull me out and

place me in His arc of safety.

And when I opened my eyes, the storm had ceased

and the atmosphere was peaceful,
and my world is beautiful.

.

Date _____

Journaling
Reflections

_____

_____

_____

_____

_____

_____

_____

_____

_____

_____

I'm praying for ....

_____

Lord teach me to....

_____

Throughout life, you meet various people.
Some of these people have a positive presence in your
life, while others don't.
Some are there with you for a lifetime, while others
are not. I appreciate the ones who had and still have
a positive presence in my life.

ATHENA GOLDSBY

My Sister

My sister is my best friend.

She is always there to lend a helping hand.

She is my love, my soul, my joy, and my heart,

till this day we will never part.

Two peas in a pod we are...

my confidant, my shining star.

Whenever I am feeling down

she finds a way to turn my frown upside down.

My sister is my love, my soul, my joy, and my heart, till

this day we will never part.

Date _____

Journaling
Reflections

_____

_____

_____

_____

_____

_____

_____

_____

_____

_____

I'm praying for ....

_____

Lord teach me to....

_____

Reminiscing Jamaal

Thinking of the day I first saw you. Little did I know that you would be a big part of my life, but I figure you knew. From the beginning, you went out of your way to do things for me as if it was your duty. You just wanted to be there for me and be a good friend, and then you became my best friend.

Not only were you there when I needed you but you were there just because and we enjoyed being in one another's presence. I miss those times but I am thankful to have had them. You made me feel comfortable. You were careful and gentle with me; you understood me, so I had no secrets from you. You respected me and made me feel as if I were a part of you. And, as the years passed and even though you moved miles away, the bond we had kept us close. You never forgot me and I will never forget you.

R.I.P.
Jamal Salaam

Date _____

Journaling
Reflections

_____

_____

_____

_____

_____

_____

_____

_____

_____

_____

I'm praying for ....

_____

Lord teach me to....

_____

Chapter Four

Mature Love

Experiencing Love

My "first love" moved to another state during my freshman year
of college. We attempted to make it work, but it didn't work. Over
the following years, my "first love" and I would talk here and
there until, eventually, the communication stopped.

You wonder if you will ever find another to love.
But of course, romance, in some form or fashion,
occurs as you continue to experience life.

So as I got older, I experienced relationships with other people.
Some of those relationships were good and others not so good...but
you live, and you learn. As you live and you learn, there is
growth and maturity. You come into a sense of what is right and
wrong and what you want out of a relationship.

Date _____

Journaling
Reflections

_____

_____

_____

_____

_____

_____

_____

_____

_____

I'm praying for ....

_____

Lord teach me to....

_____

Purposeful Love

I am yours and you are mine together forever
we are intertwined in this romance called love.
We are absorbed overwhelmingly with a passion
that all at least once in their lifetime search for.
Though some imagine finding real love...
love is not just a fantasy, love is real.
Love is being what you need me to be,
what you want me to be.
Love is purposeful with inspiration and motivation.
I purpose to love you and
I love you with the purpose of loving you forever.

Date _____

Journaling
Reflections

_____

_____

_____

_____

_____

_____

_____

_____

_____

I'm praying for ....

_____

Lord teach me to....

_____

You Are

La La La La Laaaaaa

La La La La La

La La La

La La Laaaaa

I see you smiling at me

and it's so beautiful, beautiful, beautiful.

You're in everything that I see

for my mind is stayed upon thee.

Baby, you are just too incomparable.

Mystified love keeps me on my toes.

The love you give, I feel it all in my soul,

taking me places that I've never known; through and

beyond, back to where love begun.

It's like new love and we're falling in love all over again

and it's so beautiful, beautiful, beautiful.

You are beautiful, beautiful, beautiful.

Date _____

Journaling
Reflections

_____

_____

_____

_____

_____

_____

_____

_____

_____

I'm praying for ....

_____

Lord teach me to....

_____

To Love You

What is love when there is no one to love?

What is life when there is no one to share it with? What
is a hug when there is no one to embrace? What is time
when there is no one to spend it with? What is joy when
there is no sunshine?

what is happiness when there is no you?

For to be with you is my destiny.

To love you is my profession.

My love for you is not unexplainable.

It is like chains wrapped around my heart,

which beats profoundly with every thought of you. It is
like rivers that never run dry.

It's like springtime symbolizing a new beginning. There is
no love like the love you give

and there is no joy like the joy you bring.

Date _____

Journaling
Reflections

_____

_____

_____

_____

_____

_____

_____

_____

_____

_____

I'm praying for ....

_____

Lord teach me to....

_____

Love Escapade

Come and take my hand
as we travel to a distant land,
where our bodies intertwine
as we indulge ourselves in the drink of passion.
Let the power of love ease your mind
and overtake your soul,
while our bodies become whole.
Come, come, and make love to me.
Make my heart beat as a horse's gallop.

Date _____

Journaling

How do you feel today

_____

_____

_____

_____

_____

_____

_____

_____

_____

I'm praying for ....

_____

Lord teach me to....

_____

ove

A love on cloud nine; a love eager to be mine.

A love that desires me, a love that loves tenderly.

Tender to the touch, Love caresses me.

Love romances me as we groove to a beautiful song. United with Love

in holy matrimony,

Love is my one and only.

Love has given to me a beautiful song,

Love holds me in loving arms.

Love sees the tears I cry,

Love wipes every tear from my eye.

Love is comforting.

Love listens to my most intimate thoughts

and is considerate of my every feeling.

Love is understanding.

Love is my world and I live in Love.

Love, Love, Love all around me,

Love from my head to my toes.

Love, Love, Love is all I know.

Date _____

Journaling
Reflections

_____

_____

_____

_____

_____

_____

_____

_____

_____

I'm praying for ....

_____

Lord teach me to....

_____

Chapter Five

Finding Myself

Finding Purpose

As life goes on, you question the meaning of life,
of your life.

What is my purpose?

This is the question I have on my journey.

Within

But within myself,
I am who I want to be.
I can go wherever I want to go.

Within myself, I can travel beyond
as far as the east is from the west.
I can imagine the unimaginable.

My greatest pleasure is being within myself. Here I am free.
Here everything is perfect; but as I open my eyes,
outside of myself, I am in a place I don't want to be,

I long to travel to distant lands.
Outside of myself, there is the realization of pain,
and nothing is perfect.

Date _____

Journaling
Reflections

_____

_____

_____

_____

_____

_____

_____

_____

_____

_____

I'm praying for ....

_____

Lord teach me to....

_____

Battle Within

Strife, like a spark to a flame.

Hate, a flaming rage fire of

consuming the souls thereof.

War is a weapon of mass destruction

on a battlefield of death.

Billows of smoke piercing breaths from bodies.

Date _____

Journaling
Reflections

_____

_____

_____

_____

_____

_____

_____

_____

_____

I'm praying for ....

_____

Lord teach me to....

_____

uicide

Contemplating suicide, contemplating taking my life.

The pressure from a guilty conscience is taking me under,

the pressures of life all too common.

Needing a sigh of relief, but the tension is gripping my heart.

I just don't have any peace.

My heart is racing, I can't catch my breath.

I feel I'm about to die. There is no more room left to think as I cry.

Life seems to go up and down.

Negative circumstances and situations arise.

Why, and who is to blame?

Date _____

Journaling
Reflections

_____

_____

_____

_____

_____

_____

_____

_____

_____

_____

I'm praying for ....

_____

Lord teach me to....

_____

For When you change your focus from trying to find love in and acceptance in a man, and turn your focus to cultivating a relationship with God, then you realize your reason for existing. You find that loving yourself is just as important as loving others.

ATHENA GOLDSBY

I am Somebody

I am somebody
not because of the way you make me feel,
but this is something I know to be real.

I am somebody
not because you told me so,
but this is something I just know.

I am Somebody
not because I have many friends or even big dividends,
but it's something that's within.

I don't live to fulfill your expectations because greater is He
that is in me, and His thoughts are higher than yours or mine.

Date _____

Journaling
Reflections

_____

_____

_____

_____

_____

_____

_____

_____

_____

I'm praying for ....

_____

Lord teach me to....

_____

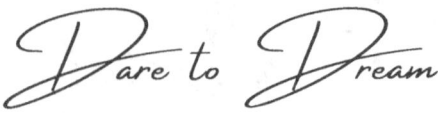

Dare to Dream

They call me the dreamer.

They say that I'm chasing clouds; that I need to come back to reality and put foolish things to the side.
Naysayers, dream killers, unbelievers, doubters, who perceive not the greatness that is within me.
Yet, I see, and this vision is from above.

This greatness is from above, illuminating my entire existence, lighting the pathway from vision to fulfillment.

Dreams of building up.

Dreams of surpassing boundaries.

Dreams of leaping over mountains.

God has disclosed to me the power in the ability to dream,

the power of perseverance, the power of being unique,

the power of seeing my life through the eyes of the greater one, and the power of believing.

God has shown me what's foolish can confound the wise.

God has revealed to me whom I am meant to be.

Now I know that being great is my destiny.

Date _____

Journaling
Reflections

_____
_____
_____
_____
_____
_____
_____
_____
_____
_____

I'm praying for ....

_____

Lord teach me to....

_____

Anew

I was in a dark place,
but you came into my life and brought light.
This light broke through my window of pain.

The reflections of what used to be shattering before me.
Yes, the broken glass shattered on the floor,
the old me is no more!
Never have I felt so free,
thank you, Lord, for your light guiding me.

No longer bound by darkness
and no longer tormented by pain.
The anger has subsided, God's love has provided.

Broken and rebuilt,
renewed and equipped...
the reflections of what used to be,
now beholding a new me!

Date _____

Journaling
Reflections

_____

_____

_____

_____

_____

_____

_____

_____

_____

_____

I'm praying for ....

_____

Lord teach me to....

_____

Radiance

---

Light comes into the world.
Jesus says I am not of this world, even as He is not of it.
God, is the Father of light, and I am made in his image,
a reflection of perfection.
He is in me, and I am in Him.
Though I am in the world, I am not of this world.
You see, I am more than what the eye can see,
and this world, it cannot contain me.
Like the sun shining bright,
just like the sun, I too contain light.

Power within me and power flowing out of me,
like the sun giving energy.
Sitting high above the horizon, just like the sun,
my gravitational force is so powerful; a force that
motivates; motivate to levitate, where mortal bodies don't
go. To the place where the knowledge of God resides and
transpires supernatural abilities that manifest limitless
achievements.
You see, I am more than what the eye can see,
and this world cannot contain me.

Date _____

Journaling
Reflections

_____

_____

_____

_____

_____

_____

_____

_____

_____

I'm praying for ....

_____

Lord teach me to....

_____

God's Word

Soul inspired. Soul derived.

God gave me those words in a dream.

We know that every scripture is God-breathed,

and His Word is strong and firm,

an everlasting foundation.

Without words there would be no life,

for God spoke and created life.

God's word is my destiny.

It has the power to control what happens in my life.

A genealogy of faith, God's Word

and faith are interconnected, right?

You confess with your mouth and with your heart you

believe, You call those things that are not,

to be as though they were.

Soul inspired, Soul derived,

God's Word in me keeps my dreams alive,

God's Word in me keeps my dreams alive.

The Psalms say, "Hope deferred makes the heart sick,"

but I say no hope at all is like a death wish.

So, I keep my mind on my Savior,

I keep my mind on my paper.

I keep my mind on my Savior.

I keep my mind on my paper, and keep pushing the pen,

cause every word I write, comes from deep within.

Every word I write comes from deep within.

God's Word in me keeps my dreams alive.

God's Word in me keeps my dreams alive.

Sharper than any double-edged sword,

God's Word is my fight, gripping every fear

and eliminating every doubt.

God's Word in me, keeps my dreams alive.

God's Word in me, keeps my dreams alive.

Date _____

Journaling
Reflections

_____

_____

_____

_____

_____

_____

_____

_____

_____

I'm praying for ....

_____

Lord teach me to....

_____

Faith

Faith, a most prized possession.

Like a family heirloom

that is passed from generation to generation.

A safely kept treasure,

keeping alive hope and keeping families together.

Date _____

Journaling
Reflections

_____

_____

_____

_____

_____

_____

_____

_____

_____

_____

I'm praying for ....

_____

Lord teach me to....

_____

On the Wings of my Savior

Wondering, wondering, wondering, in this lost world.

Getting by each day on a hope, on a hope that one day

I will fly, on the wings of my Savior,

eyes closed hands to the sky.

Whoever said that it would be easy

surely these winds blow hard at times.

Praying for strength that I won't let go,

I got to keep my eye on the prize.

I'm flying high...I'm flying high, on the wings of my Savior.

Mounted up with wings like eagles

high above the clouds and guided by your love.

I'm flying high...I'm flying high, on the wings of my Savior.

Date _____

Journaling
Reflections

_____

_____

_____

_____

_____

_____

_____

_____

_____

I'm praying for ....

_____

Lord teach me to....

_____

Everything

Everything, everything, is it really what it seems?

Wanting to experience life and all it must bring.

Everything, everything, isn't perfect,

but I'm dying to live my life with purpose.

Everything, everything, is it really what it seems?

Wanting to experience life and fulfill all my dreams.

Date _____

Journaling
Reflections

_____

_____

_____

_____

_____

_____

_____

_____

_____

I'm praying for ....

_____

Lord teach me to....

_____

When I found you

You beckoned me to you.

You told me to seek you, and I shall find you.

Rebirth; a better me.

Death in Christ, raised to life in Christ; raised with purpose.

Finding myself in You, the meaning of

"You are my purpose;"

"You are my purpose,"

The meaning of finding myself in You...

I found myself when I found you.

Date _____

Journaling
Reflections

_____

_____

_____

_____

_____

_____

_____

_____

_____

I'm praying for ....

_____

Lord teach me to....

_____

Conclusion

Your "first love" is and should be God Almighty. This has been my growth over the years. My focus shifted from searching and seeking to find love and acceptance from a man, to seeking a deeper relationship with God. The more I came to know God, the more intimacy with Him I desired. The presence of God strengthened me. Over the course of writing, I never thought or could see that God was working and using the creativity he had given me for a purpose. Though I may be confined to a wheelchair physically, mentally I have no limitations. He showed me that He is still able to use me for His Glory. God Almighty showed me that in Him, I can achieve anything. I say to you, that in God, you can achieve anything!

Exodus 31:2-3

"Look, I have specifically chosen Bezalel son of Uri, grandson of Hur, of the tribe of Judah. I have filled him with the Spirit of God, giving him great wisdom, ability, and expertise in all kinds of crafts." New Living Translation

Journal

Express Yourself

My daily prayer

Today's Scriptures

Lord teach me to.... _____

_____

_____

_____

_____

_____

_____

_____

thank you

I'm praying for ....

prayer requests

_____
_____
_____
_____
_____
_____
_____
_____

reflections

_____
_____
_____
_____
_____
_____
_____
_____

things on my heart

Amen

my daily prayer

Today's Scriptures

Lord teach me to....

_____
_____
_____
_____
_____
_____
_____

thank you

I'm praying for ....

prayer requests

_____
_____
_____
_____
_____
_____
_____

reflections

_____
_____
_____
_____
_____
_____
_____

things on my heart

Amen

my daily prayer

Today's Scriptures

Lord teach me to....

_____

_____

_____

_____

_____

_____

_____

thank you

I'm praying for ....

prayer requests

_____
_____
_____
_____
_____
_____
_____
_____

reflections

_____
_____
_____
_____
_____
_____
_____
_____
_____

things on my heart

Amen

my daily prayer
Today's Scriptures

Lord teach me to....

_____

_____

_____

_____

_____

_____

_____

_____

thank you

I'm praying for ....

prayer requests

_____

_____

_____

_____

_____

_____

_____

_____

reflections

_____

_____

_____

_____

_____

_____

_____

things on my heart

_____

_____

Amen

_____

my daily prayer
Today's Scriptures

Lord teach me to....

_____
_____
_____
_____
_____
_____
_____

thank you

I'm praying for ....

prayer requests

_____
_____
_____
_____
_____
_____
_____

reflections

_____
_____
_____
_____
_____
_____
_____
_____

things on my heart

Amen

my daily prayer

Today's Scriptures

Lord teach me to....

_____

_____

_____

_____

_____

_____

_____

_____

thank you

I'm praying for ....

prayer requests

_____

_____

_____

_____

_____

_____

_____

reflections

_____

_____

_____

_____

_____

_____

_____

things on my heart

_____

_____

Amen

my daily prayer

Today's Scriptures

Lord teach me to....

_____

_____

_____

_____

_____

_____

_____

thank you

I'm praying for ....

prayer requests

_____
_____
_____
_____
_____
_____
_____
_____

reflections

_____
_____
_____
_____
_____
_____
_____
_____

things on my heart

Amen

my daily prayer
Today's Scriptures

Lord teach me to....

_____

_____

_____

_____

_____

_____

_____

thank you

I'm praying for ....

prayer requests

_____

_____

_____

_____

_____

_____

_____

reflections

_____

_____

_____

_____

_____

things on my heart

_____

_____

_____

Amen

my daily prayer
Today's Scriptures

Lord teach me to....

_____
_____
_____
_____
_____
_____
_____
_____

thank you

I'm praying for ....

prayer requests

_____

_____

_____

_____

_____

_____

_____

_____

reflections

_____

_____

_____

_____

_____

_____

things on my heart

_____

_____

_____

Amen

my daily prayer

Today's Scriptures

Lord teach me to....

_____

_____

_____

_____

_____

_____

_____

thank you

I'm praying for ....

prayer requests

_____
_____
_____
_____
_____
_____
_____

reflections

_____
_____
_____
_____
_____
_____
_____

things on my heart

Amen

my daily prayer

Today's Scriptures

Lord teach me to....

_____

_____

_____

_____

_____

_____

_____

thank you

I'm praying for ....

prayer requests

_____
_____
_____
_____
_____
_____
_____
_____

reflections

_____
_____
_____
_____
_____
_____
_____
_____

things on my heart

Amen

my daily prayer

Today's Scriptures

Lord teach me to....

_____

_____

_____

_____

_____

_____

_____

thank you

I'm praying for ....

prayer requests

_____
_____
_____
_____
_____
_____
_____
_____

reflections

_____
_____
_____
_____
_____
_____
_____
_____
_____
_____

things on my heart

Amen

my daily prayer

Today's Scriptures

Lord teach me to....

_____

_____

_____

_____

_____

_____

_____

thank you

I'm praying for ....

prayer requests

_____
_____
_____
_____
_____
_____
_____
_____

reflections

_____
_____
_____
_____
_____
_____
_____
_____

things on my heart

Amen

my daily prayer

Today's Scriptures

Lord teach me to....

_____
_____
_____
_____
_____
_____
_____
_____

thank you

I'm praying for ....

prayer requests

_____

_____

_____

_____

_____

_____

_____

_____

reflections

_____

_____

_____

_____

_____

_____

_____

things on my heart

Amen

my daily prayer

Today's Scriptures

Lord teach me to....

_____
_____
_____
_____
_____
_____
_____

thank you

I'm praying for ....

prayer requests

_____

_____

_____

_____

_____

_____

_____

reflections

_____

_____

_____

_____

_____

_____

_____

things on my heart

_____

_____

Amen

my daily prayer

Today's Scriptures

Lord teach me to....

_____

_____

_____

_____

_____

_____

_____

_____

thank you

I'm praying for ....

prayer requests

_____
_____
_____
_____
_____
_____
_____

reflections

_____
_____
_____
_____
_____
_____
_____
_____
_____

things on my heart

Amen

my daily prayer

Today's Scriptures

Lord teach me to....

_____

_____

_____

_____

_____

_____

_____

thank you

I'm praying for ....

prayer requests

_____
_____
_____
_____
_____
_____
_____
_____

reflections

_____
_____
_____
_____
_____
_____
_____
_____

things on my heart

Amen

my daily prayer

Today's Scriptures

Lord teach me to....

_____

_____

_____

_____

_____

_____

_____

_____

thank you

I'm praying for ....

prayer requests

_____

_____

_____

_____

_____

_____

_____

reflections

_____

_____

_____

_____

_____

_____

things on my heart

_____

_____

Amen

my daily prayer

Today's Scriptures

Lord teach me to....

_____
_____
_____
_____
_____
_____
_____

thank you

I'm praying for ....

prayer requests

_____

_____

_____

_____

_____

_____

_____

reflections

_____

_____

_____

_____

_____

_____

_____

things on my heart

_____

_____

Amen

my daily prayer

Today's Scriptures

Lord teach me to....

_____

_____

_____

_____

_____

_____

_____

thank you

I'm praying for ....

prayer requests

_____
_____
_____
_____
_____
_____
_____
_____

reflections

_____
_____
_____
_____
_____
_____
_____

things on my heart

Amen

_____

my daily prayer
Today's Scriptures

Lord teach me to....

_____

_____

_____

_____

_____

_____

_____

thank you

I'm praying for ....

prayer requests

_____

_____

_____

_____

_____

_____

_____

reflections

_____

_____

_____

_____

_____

_____

_____

_____

things on my heart

_____

_____

Amen

my daily prayer

Today's Scriptures

Lord teach me to....

_____

_____

_____

_____

_____

_____

_____

thank you

I'm praying for ....

prayer requests

_____
_____
_____
_____
_____
_____
_____
_____

reflections

_____
_____
_____
_____
_____
_____
_____

things on my heart

Amen

my daily prayer

Today's Scriptures

Lord teach me to....

_____
_____
_____
_____
_____
_____
_____
_____

thank you

I'm praying for ....

prayer requests

_____
_____
_____
_____
_____
_____
_____

reflections

_____
_____
_____
_____
_____
_____
_____

things on my heart

Amen

my daily prayer

Today's Scriptures

Lord teach me to....

_____

_____

_____

_____

_____

_____

_____

_____

thank you

I'm praying for ....

ATHENA GOLDSBY

VISIONFROMABOVE.TODAY/

Athena Goldsby is a native of Farmerville, Louisiana. she graduated high school in 2002. She attended Grambling State University from 2002-2015, where she received her BS in Computer Information Systems and her Master's in Criminal Justice.

Upon graduating in 2015, Athena obtained a job in the legal field, working as a Legal Assistant. Decades prior to graduating from college, Athena was shot and subsequently paralyzed. It was then, in 1998, that Athena began writing poetry. Writing became therapy until she lost her favorite journal given to her by a friend. In losing her journal, she realized that her writings were meaningful and purposeful. Writing gave her peace, joy, and encouragement so she prayed to God that He would help her find her journal and open doors to have them published. The prayers were answered, and her mother found her journal while cleaning.

Athena began writing again, and her first poem from there was entitled, "Dare to Dream," which was given to her through the Spirit of God one day as she was reading about Joseph being sold into slavery by his brother. Ms. Goldsby is encouraged to walk in her God-given gift and wants to encourage others to do the same.

Welcome

Founders of Living Water Books Publishing Company

Visit our website Livingwaterbooks.org

My husband Charles and I are the founders of Living Water Books Christian Publishing Company. I always knew from my childhood that I was chosen to record (write) for God. The prophetic gift rested upon my mother. My father told me I had the spiritual gift, but I needed to learn the skill, so he admonished me to pursue a higher education. I began college courses while in high school and three years later I received my B.A. Degree in Mass Communications with a concentration in News Editorial, Broadcasting, and Journalism. I met my husband and a few years later I released my first book, A Heart Unraveled, which I self-published. It became a best-seller allowing us to travel doing conferences, interviews, and book signings.

God established our business on the foundations of (John 7:38), Whoever believes in me, as scripture has said, rivers of living water will flow from within them. Living Water being symbolic for Holy Spirit living within us became the Living Waters within our writings as we prepared resources for our marriage ministry. Holy Spirit splashed through the pages and the testimonies that derived from the resources told us what we needed to do next. We looked at one another and said the name will be,
Living Water Books.

> " Living Water Books is God's company. The Living Water of God into books distributed all over the world. God chose us as stewards and we are committed to serving God's Kingdom through God's people. "

Living Water Books
John 7:38

CONTACT US TODAY

THE CHRISTIAN
PUBLISHING COMPANY

WEBSITE: LIVINGWATERBOOKS.ORG